THE Seasons OF
Breaking Free

♡ LisA...
thank you for
Always being there
for me!
♡ Morgan

MORGAN NUCILLI

ISBN 978-1-0980-6017-6 (paperback)
ISBN 978-1-0980-6018-3 (digital)

Christian Faith Publishing, Inc.
832 Park Avenue
Meadville, PA 16335
www.christianfaithpublishing.com

Printed in the United States of America

To my late mother

"Share each other's burdens, and in this way
obey the law of Christ."
—Galatians 6:2

In this book, I will be discussing the different seasons we as Christians experience. Each moment can bring sadness or joy. We experience different emotions as we live each day. I want to share with you the last four years of my life. I will be open and honest, but I will share with you even in the midst of your darkest day, God will show up. I will be sharing scripture that has helped in my most difficult and darkest time. I encourage you to take time to soak in the word and journal with the pages offered at the end of each chapter.

Whether you are married, single, young, old, a sister, a mother, a daughter, etc., you have had, will, or know someone that has experienced the moments that I will be discussing. I encourage you to pray before the beginning of each chapter to get in the presence of God. Have joy in the journey and be an encourager to others along the way. Even when you are asking yourself what more can I take, He will show you that you are not alone. You must remain humble to yourself and His word.

Humbling yourself in sad times can sometimes be the hardest thing you can do. Having peace in the waiting can feel like time has stopped and no one is listening. These are the moments that you are living second by second, then you move to minute by minute, but trusting Him and His word, you will be able to live, day by day. By the end of this book, I want you to look at the season in which you are in and be able to praise Him in your waiting.

Remember that praying is an exchange. Give God your worries, and he will give you His Grace. Instead of worrying about anything, pray about everything. You will be able to feel the weight come off your chest and physically feel the tenseness be lifted from your shoulders. Go to war in your storm and make praying a lifestyle. It can and will truly save your life.

> "Cast all your anxiety on him because he cares for you."
>
> —1 Peter 5:7

CONTENTS

Chapter 1: The Season of Empathy..............................9
Chapter 2: The Season of Disappointment 18
Chapter 3: The Season of Darkness 25
Chapter 4: The Season of Brokenness 32
Chapter 5: The Season of Uncertainty 41
Chapter 6: The Season of Obedience 48
Chapter 7: The Season of Praise..............................54
Chapter 8: The Season of Trust..............................59
Chapter 9: The Season of Faith..............................65

CHAPTER 1

THE SEASON OF EMPATHY

"Rejoice with those who rejoice, weep with those who weep."

—Romans 12:15

Empathy. What does empathy mean to you? Do you feel sorry for another? Do you truly feel other's pain and sadness, as if you were the one experiencing the moment? I was the definition of empathetic. A mother, a teacher, and a wife. I wiped noses, tended to boo-boos, and was always making sure everyone else was satisfied, fed, and felt loved. Being empathetic became more than a feeling in my stomach or a sadness in my heart. It had taken over my life. It was who I had become, who I was, and who I thought I was always going to be.

I remember my morning prayer would begin like this, "Dear Lord, please wrap your arms of protection around my family. Keep them safe and warm. And please, Lord, do not let me have to live a day without my husband. Amen." I had lost my father to a massive heart attack at the young age of forty-six. He was here one moment and gone the absolute next. The fear of death had consumed my life, and I was fearful that everyone I loved would be taken from me as quickly as my father.

I was angry and confused. At the age of twenty, my focus was on myself, my friends, and not God. I filled my life with empty pleasures and consumed my days on trying to work three jobs and was attending college full time. Upon completing my college degree and getting my first teaching job, my life quickly changed when I found out I was going to have a baby. I was a mom at that very moment, and I had a job to protect her. The moment I gave birth to my daughter, I quickly knew life was changed forever. My days were going to be filled with love, laughter, and I hoped to show her who God was. And I did just that, when I could. I took her to church when I had the energy. With that being said, I didn't make it a priority, but I had every intention to do so.

I was a preschool teacher at the time. I had a classroom of eighteen four-year-olds, four days a week, cleaning and lesson plans on Friday, and the weekends would pass so quickly. I tried to consume our weekends with family time and fun. There was one thing that made my heart happy and full of joy, and it was my husband. I had met him in 2005 while attending college. I was a lost Christian and consumed my time and days with him from that moment on. I loved him more than words could explain. Like most young couples, we had so much to learn, but we both loved our baby girl more than we loved ourselves.

I continued to live my life for others, and I was happy with that. But one day, I realized how extremely exhausted I had become. I would catch myself thinking not nice thoughts after people wouldn't thank me or I would get so hurt by the littlest actions of others. I wasn't sure what was going on, but I knew that I was starting to feel different. I discussed this feeling with my husband, and together, we blamed lack of sleep and hormones. I continued to push through each day with a smile, and I continued to show my family unconditional love. I knew that I did not want my family to ever have unanswered questions or concerns as to if I had loved them.

And to ensure this, I wanted to make their lives easier. I did this by creating an ideal environment for everyone around me. I made it easier for everyone to be engaged in their own world and their own thoughts, so deeply that I got lost along the way. Have you ever felt like this? Are you tired of pleasing others, but not getting any positive reaction in return? I felt that way too, and one day in particular, I remember knowing that I wasn't okay.

It had been an extremely long week. I had a child in my class that was experiencing situations at home that I never had experienced or couldn't even imagine enduring. I had spent hours of prepping the child with a backpack full of food to make sure he would be fed during the upcoming school break. I remember coming home to my warm, nice, and clean home. I was so grateful. I walked in, and I saw my healthy sleeping daughter on the couch being watched by her beloved grandfather. I had very little worries in my life, but I was tired. I started the shower and began weeping. I was empty. When sharing my emotions and feelings with my mom, she told me she would pray for me. I remember thanking her, but I wasn't sold that a prayer would fix my issues. I felt selfish for even having these feelings and thoughts when others struggled and hurt. My problems were so small for God.

Moments went by quickly, days turned into weeks, and weeks into years. I continued working as a preschool teacher, and we were blessed to receive news of having another child. I gave birth to my second child, a son. I knew in my heart that he was going to complete our family and our days would be filled with love and memories for years to come. I continued to try to keep life positive and everyone happy, but I always messed up. Somehow. I would have everything planned perfectly, but something would always mess up my plans. Instead of being encouraged for the effort, I felt that I was unappreciated, and it would frustrate me. I had not ever allowed myself to feel this way. I continued to blame myself and my hormones, and I just didn't know what was wrong with me. I didn't want to bother anyone with the way I was feeling, so I kept it to myself. Ending in a result of feeling even more empty and alone.

One night, I was struggling to shut my mind off while I was attempting to go to sleep. I remember finally closing my eyes and pleading with myself. Thankfully, I drifted off, but I quickly entered a reoccurring dream. It was the same as before. The dream was in black and white. I was holding a baby and was being chased by a man. Instead of escaping through the front door, I always chose the stairs. They would wind and spiral, and I could always feel him right behind me. I would always wake up at the exact same moment, every time. He would grab my arm, and before I could turn around, I would wake. My heart was racing, and I was sweating. I couldn't calm down. So I remember thinking, maybe a drink of water would help.

So I slipped out of bed, checking on each child as I passed their bedrooms. I had made it to the kitchen, and my heartrate had finally calmed down, but I couldn't shake a nervous feeling. Normally, I would quickly return to bed, and quietly drift back to sleep. But this night was different. I knew I wasn't ready for that; quietly, I sat down at the table and still could not shake the unsettling feeling lingering from my dream. I started googling dreams and the meaning of certain colors, but nothing made me feel better. So I decided to do something I had not done in some time. I bowed my head and I began speaking to a stranger. I felt ashamed, embarrassed, and I was unsure what to even say. I knew He loved me, and I knew He remembered who I was. But after my dad had passed, I had allowed anger to consume me. I said things to God that I should not have said. I was ashamed and scared that He would not forgive me. But I remembered what my great-grandmother would always say, "He doesn't care how far you have strayed, He will always welcome you back in His arms." And in this moment, I didn't know what else to do.

I remember bowing my head, folding my hands, and I began praying for peace and guidance. I then made my way to the floor and began to weep. My heart was speaking, but my mouth wasn't moving. I was asking for forgiveness of my sins and apologized for being so angry and blaming him of my father's death. I apologized for the moment I yelled at Him when I was hugging my forty-six-year-old father in his casket. I apologized for asking Him where He was and why He would allow my kind, hardworking father to not have a chance, but He allowed murderers and mean people to live.

I held my hands up and I said, "God, I am broken. I am scared. And I am sad. Please help me." I heard nothing, but the peace that began to fill me was something that I cannot humanly explain. I felt calm and warm with a feeling of love and contentment. I wanted more but had no idea how to make this happen. I lifted myself up from the floor and made my way back to bed. I lay down, feeling better than I had in years. And like I had done time and time again, I promised myself and Him that I wouldn't wait so long to talk to Him again. I didn't want to wait until I was broken to pray again. I wanted to pray each day and begin going to church more regularly.

I truly desired a relationship with God, but life was just so busy. I eventually went back to only praying when I had a hard moment or bad day. God would remind me that He was there and would fill me with a love and feeling that I had never received from anyone but Him. But life kept moving, and I wasn't faithful to my promise that I had made to God on that dark night.

Being raised in church and hearing God's word from my grandparents and mother, I knew that was the lifestyle that I wanted and needed, not only for me but for my family. But I didn't realize that it would be such hard work. I didn't discipline myself and felt as if I kept running away from Him instead of toward Him. But I knew that I needed my relationship with God, Jesus Christ, and the Holy Spirit. I needed to find a church home and I needed more for myself and my family to survive the lonely season of empathy.

I had given so much of myself to everyone else that I didn't recognize the person in the mirror. Have you ever asked yourself, how can I manage my family's emotions, wants, and needs if I can't even manage my own? This is when the love of Jesus and the love of yourself needs to grow. Without a healthy relationship with God, your inner conflicts are not salvable, and they will only be punishable. I was blaming myself for everything negative in my life, without recognizing myself for any of the positives. I was begging for my loved ones to recognize and show appreciation, but that is not what I needed. They loved me, and I knew they loved me, but I didn't realize it at this moment.

I needed to look at myself like God looks at me. He gave us the ability to have positive self-reflection and self-control. Positive self-reflection is a skill that allows us to put a pause in between our impulse. For example, if you are angry and your immediate reaction is to pick up whatever is in front of you and throw it, that is an impulse. We all have impulses, but they can be in different forms.

Power of the Pause!

For an example, an impulse could be hurtful words, yelling, or any type of action that you may soon regret. When you have a good relationship with God, He gives you the power to pause. You don't react immediately but instead you pause. In this pause, you can pray or just take a breath before you speak or react in the moment. When you develop this power of the pause, life will change for the positive.

I knew that I wanted to be spiritually alive and to grow in my walk with God. I knew my body was a shell and I didn't have to be a slave to the devil or the enemy of self-pity. I knew this because my grandmother had prayed this prayer for me as a child. She prayed I would know my self-worth and I would never feel unloved. As a young child, I didn't know what those words meant, but they stayed with me, and each time I would pray, even the smallest prayer I would hear these words. I knew the first step for closing the season of empathy was to allow God to work in my life. Jesus will set you free, and He will change you from the inside out, but He will do this if only you allow it. I knew that I needed to be intentional in my walk with Him and that it was not going to be easy.

It was not going to be easy because I was a worrier. I always carried the weight of the world on my shoulders and wore my heart on my sleeve. I was sensitive and an empathic. I didn't know how to not worry. My family was worriers, and this I knew because they would talk about it. They would stress about things before they even occurred. They prepared for the worst, and because of this generational curse, I was living this way as well. Not until I started this walk with God did I know that I can break this cycle for my children. I finally knew what it meant when people would tell me, don't worry about it, just give it to God. He wants us to be obedient, and He desires a relationship with us. How incredible is it that God desires a relationship with you!

I would like for you to stop at this moment and repeat this prayer with me. "Dear heavenly Father, I give it to you, Oh Lord. I pray against any fear, strongholds, resentment, and anger that I may have. I pray that you help me to still love and care for others but allow me to love myself as well. I am thankful. I am grateful. I am sorry for my sins, in Jesus's name, Amen."

Are you willing to allow Him to do His work in you? Are you willing to have peace in your situation? Your life? Your friendships or marriage? Sin is contagious, but thankfully, Jesus is greater than sin. He has already paid the price so we can live free from sin and have eternal life. If Jesus is willing to restore His relationship with you, I am willing to bow to Him. Fear cannot control me. Guilt can no longer have a hold on my life. I know I am a carrier of His love.

Do not give in to sin, do not give out in fear, and do not give up on yourself. God loves the humble. Stay humble and know He is a good Father. We were all born blind to sin. We had to see God in our lives, at our own time to grow in faith with Him. Do not make Him our problem like I did. I allowed the lie of the enemy during my father's death to control my relationship with God.

God is easy to blame, but He is not the problem; He is the answer. We are not expected to understand the "no" in the moment, but we are expected to control our actions and our heart. In trying moments, we must focus on the solution, which is God, instead of the problem, which is sin. Sin causes us to be blind, and the sin of the world will allow us to not see clearly. This is what carried me to my next season.

The season of disappointment. This is when we have unrealistic expectations about a person or situation and without faith, it can result in disappointment. Disappointment can lead you to feeling fear, unloved, and undeserving.

"The good person out of the good treasure of the heart produces good, and the evil person out of evil treasure produces evil; for it is out of the abundance of the heart that the mouth speaks."

—Luke 6:45

Minute Motivation

Take a few minutes and write what comes
to mind. Do not overthink it.

What should I spend more time doing?	Why don't I?	What can't I do to be able to?
Prayer Word Exercise Loving my family		

Soak in His Word and Share Your Thoughts!

CHAPTER 2

THE SEASON OF DISAPPOINTMENT

"Have patience, God isn't finished yet."
—Philippians 1:6

Have you ever been in the middle of a conversation or action, and something in that moment brings a negative thought to your mind? Maybe it wasn't the exact same situation but something from that moment makes you think about an experience that was once negative? This experience, moment, or word made such a powerful impact on your life that even the thought takes you back to that moment. For example, there is an event that happens in my town every year. On that event date each year, it takes me back to the night when I first realized that divorce might be in my future.

That moment of disappointment was one of the most hurtful and negative moments of my life up to this point. The same empty feeling that I had once experienced had crept back in my life in an instant. My world stopped, and I began to be consumed with trying to collect moments, conversations, and situations that led up to this moment. I began pouring self-doubt, blame, and sadness on my situation. Not once did I speak life, truth, or love into this moment. I was mad. I was sad and, above all, frustrated. I could not shake it. This cloud of darkness followed me for the next six months. I had not shared this with anyone, I was trying to deal with it on my own, but it literally began to tear me apart.

My once empathic personality now felt selfish and shameful. I again felt unlovable, unimportant, and unworthy of God's love. I was struggling financially and spiritually. I had given up my growing relationship with God, and I allowed the enemy to fill my head, heart, and life with worldly advice. The separation from my husband felt as if I was experiencing another death, a grieving experience unlike any other. Grieving the presence of a living soul that you loved more than you loved yourself. The hurt that I was experiencing was unexplainable. I had an array of emotions, but the one that was most impactful was the feeling of disappointment. Disappointment of now experiencing a life that I did not want and I did not believe in, but I was broken and lost.

I felt as if I were failing my children and I again blamed it on God. How could God forsake my family? How could He allow this to happen to us? I was pointing my finger at Him and shaking it fiercely, full of anger and confusion. But not until one day did I hear Him plainly say, "How could I be to blame when your marriage didn't have me in it?"

What? He didn't feel like He was in my marriage, but I prayed, and my children prayed, and we went to church each Sunday. Well, every other Sunday. And my body was there, but maybe my mind was watching others or thinking about what we were going to do later in the day. This was the reality of the moment when I asked myself, "Had I really not allowed God in my marriage?"

I know my husband and I did not share the same thoughts on religion, but that was just because we were raised in different religious cultures, which didn't make him right or me wrong. We were just different, which was okay, but what wasn't okay was that we, as a couple, did not make God the center of our marriage. We allowed our differences in religion to not unite our marriage to include God. What could we have done differently? Do you ever catch yourself asking, what if? What could I have done differently?

Not only had my marriage failed, but now I had the disappointment and the burden of knowing that by not allowing God in, He wasn't there when we needed Him. The question: Could our problems be worked out? Do you ever wonder if miscommunication between you and your spouse is the problem in your marriage? I am the first to tell you that I tried to do it all on my own. I didn't want to bother him, I wanted to fix everything for us, but my husband wasn't even made aware of the problem. Could this misbehavior on my part lead into a missing skill, which results in miscommunication?

Be very cautious of this. All behavior is a form of communication. What you think you are saying with your words can be received completely different because of your actions. My state or my behavior can dictate your behavior. For example, if I come home in a bad mood because of a coworker and my husband comes home in a good mood. My grumpy actions and negative behavior can carry into my interaction with him. When you do this, you have allowed your state of emotions to dictate your husband's state of emotion. This usually would turn into an argument, for no reason. I was lacking a skill of communication and it was hurtful to my relationship. My husband did not make me angry, but because I was already upset, maybe he triggered something under lying inside of me which makes me react in a negative way.

Having a healthy relationship with God and a strong spiritual connection can help you with your communication skills as well. Not having God in your home or relationship can affect this way of communicating dramatically. When giving the world your all but not giving your all to God, you are allowing room for the devil to enter your relationship. When this happens, your words and action can become misleading and upsetting. You can feel as if you are giving your all in your relationship and marriage, and you are not getting anything back in return. This can lead to feeling not valued or worthless. You will then begin to question your self-worth in your different relationships, and that is when room is made for resentment. Without giving this situation or relationship to God, you have allowed your expectation to be led by fear and not faith.

Once you are in the presence of God and learn how to manage yourself as a follower, everything will change. If you practice the power of the pause, your life will change in positive ways. What you once considered a disappointment could now be viewed as an opportunity. You do not have to be afraid or discouraged. You can go out and face your battles knowing that you are not alone. Once you are confident in knowing that you are not alone, you must choose to change negative thoughts and change certain patterns in life.

Ask yourself, do you want to *have peace within*? Yes, I want to have peace in my heart. Do you want to *be happy*? Yes, I want to be happy! Now, this is the first step. When you determine what you want and desire, then you can soak in His word and begin putting this practice to work. When I soak in His word, I like being in a quiet environment. I like to take notes and will end my quiet time by listening to Christian music. You set the environment as you would for anything else in your life. For example, when it is bedtime, you are not going to crank up the music and leave the lights on. You turn down the lights and lay down in a calm and peaceful environment.

My advice to you is to take a moment and invite Him in and make Him feel welcome in your heart and your home. God will then help you find the emotions you so desperately desire.

Life will take you on many different paths and you will run many races. I fell down while running my race (my marriage) which turned into the season of disappointment. But once I was down from falling, I had to make a choice. Do I stay down or do I get up and keep moving forward? I didn't allow staying down to be a choice of mine. I knew allowing the enemy to keep me down was not an option for my children and I. That is the moment I stood up, tired and weak, but I could only do this knowing God was on my side.

Remember, you hold the key to your spiritual freedom. You are in control of which lane you are going to run in. God is molding you for something more. He is developing and preparing you before He is ready to release you.

Is comfort keeping you from growing? Do you have comfort in people? Maybe the *comfort* is not all God has planned for your life. The devil can speak and make you feel comfortable, but you must allow God to disrupt that comfort. God does not come to condemn you, but He does come to confront your normal. Rebuke the devil and stop allowing him to drain your energy. Allow God to help you protect your energy and find complete comfort in God's Word and presence.

Are you where you want to be, or do you want more? My advice is to be still and listen. This is where I was during the beginning of my separation, but I had no idea what was ahead of me with the season of darkness approaching.

"The pain that you've been feeling cannot compare to the joy that's coming"
—Romans 8:18

Today is...

Today I am grateful for...	Pray for...
_____	
_____	
_____	
_____	
_____	
_____	
_____	
_____	
_____	
_____	
_____	
_____	
_____	
I have seen the hand of God in my life...	

Soak in His Word and Share Your Thoughts!

CHAPTER 3

THE SEASON OF DARKNESS

"Love your enemies. Do good to those who
hate you. Speak well of those who curse you."
—Luke 6:27–28

Darkness. Have you ever thought about darkness being a thought instead of a place? This upcoming season that I was entering was one that broke my heart but eventually was meant to fix my perspective. On days when you feel like you are in the dark, are you expecting? Are you expecting God to show up or do you assume He has forgotten about you? No one can help you with this decision, except you. Even on my darkest day, He helped me to remember the days I prayed for the things that I was blessed with right now. I knew God had a plan for me and my family, and I was anticipating the next chapter. I was ready to move forward and not look back.

The only problem was that my husband and I were still separated and nowhere close to fixing everything negative in our marriage. We had a lot of stuff that I wasn't ready to let go of. I wanted to remain faithful to God, but I couldn't make sense of why I was holding on to this resentment. I felt as if I needed to find a purpose and a reason to help me to humble myself in this situation. I needed to own my mistakes and let go of the negative memory and move on with the positives in mind. All I wanted was to be interwoven with my husband and leave the uncertainty and prepare us for God's unending grace.

Once I allowed God's guidance to show me what to do, then I was able to move past the season of disappointment. At this point, I was in a new routine with my children, but life was still hard and some days, sad. When I described my days and mood, I would describe it as a picture of a woman with a cloud above her head. You know the one I am referring to? With each step she takes, the rain continues to come down, but only on her. I felt like I had a dark cloud floating above me constantly. I felt like I was living in a storm. I would put a smile on my face to hide the tears in my eyes. I couldn't eat because I would only get sick, and I was lost. The person I shared my life and home with was in a distant. I was no longer happy, eager, independent, or creative. I was sad and full of confusion.

But one Monday morning, I received a phone call from my mother. She and I had not seen each other for a couple of weeks, and that was something we tried to not do very often. She told me that she had a doctor's appointment on Wednesday morning, and she asked if I would go with her, and then we could go get dinner. Without question, I said yes. Everyone knows what I mean when I say, no matter your age, sometimes you just need to see your mom! That is where I was. So we made our plans and we ended the conversation as normal, "I'll talk to you soon, love you!"

I lived two hours away from my mom, and I remember Wednesday morning approached quickly. I couldn't wait to see her, and I had so much to tell her. I drove and remember being consumed with my situation drowning in my own sorrows. Upon arriving to her appointment, I tried talking to God and I asked Him to give me peace while I was around my mom. I knew she worried about me, and I didn't want her to see anything less than strength and independence coming from me.

I pulled in and she was waiting on me in her car. We greeted each other with a hug and we walked in together, laughing and talking. I was greeted by an old friend, who was a nurse in the office. It was so nice to see her. We shared hugs and spoke for a few moments, but I could tell her face was very still and her presence very somber. I quickly began to move my mood to sadness for my situation to fear of the true reason of the appointment.

It was Mom's turn. I remember them announcing her name in the quiet waiting area. We walked back into a bright hallway, but all I could feel was the coldness of the walls. The smell of latex gloves is still in memory, as if I were sitting there today. The doctor came in with the same emotion on her face as I had seen on my friend. When the doctor began to speak, I heard nothing after I heard the word *cancer*. Cancer. What? My already dark, sad, and confused world stopped. I couldn't breathe. I couldn't hear or see. I looked at my mother in disbelief.

"Stage 3 breast cancer!" My eyes were fixated on my mother, and without thought, I said, "What?" Quickly followed with a very loud and abrupt, "Why?" My eyes filled with tears and my palms became clammy. I looked over at my mom who sat there in a very still position, poised yet confused. I remember wiping away the tears and whispering, "Why you, Mom, haven't we been through enough?" At that moment, with tear-filled eyes and a quivering lip, my mother looked at me and said, "Why not me, Morgan?!" I remember my eyes getting large, as I dropped my head in complete and total disbelief. A woman who I loved more than I could explain, a woman who has experienced grief firsthand more times than anyone should. More times than she ever deserved. I couldn't believe she said that. But she was right. "Why not me?" she said again.

She got up and walked over to where I was sitting. She placed her hand under my chin and made me look up at her. And she said, "But, sweetie, I choose to live because I love life." And that she did! She saw the goodness in others and had the giving heart that only I dream to have. She cared for elderly patients who suffered from dementia, but she always reminded them they were safe and made them comfortable. So I knew at this moment we only had one choice.

So I did what any daughter would do. I made the phone calls she requested, but the worst one was the one I had to make to my sister. We went to Mom's house, packed a bag, and I drove her two hours to my house. We had no idea the road that was before us, but we knew that we would be doing it together. After hours of phone calls and consultation visits, we finally had a plan in place. For the next year, my mother would be fighting for her life with chemotherapy infusions, radiation treatments, and surgery. But being new to the battle, we didn't consider the nausea, fatigue, and hair loss that was in between.

In a moment, my life full of self-pity and darkness stopped, and a season of hope and fight began. My time with my husband was less and the trying became distant on my end. My life was consumed with getting my mother healthy but life was stressful and hard, and I was tired. But complaining wasn't an option, I felt like I couldn't. I knew that my mother needed me. My father was gone, and my sister lived nine hundred miles away. I put a smile on my face and continued to put gas in the car, and we kept driving and pushing through.

But the day had come when her hair started to thin and the reality of it falling out was before us. She asked me if I would shave it for her. I remember thinking, *Haven't I done enough?* But I couldn't tell her no, and I remember praying, "God, I cannot do this on my own." With the help of my dearest friend, the task was complete, and we knew we had a big day ahead of us. We had to be at her treatment early the next morning. She was embarrassed and extremely sick from the treatment the week before. I remember getting her a wheelchair and pushing her into the treatment center. In the waiting room, she noticed a very pale, sick woman. My mother wanted to pray for her. My eyes filled with tears, and at that moment, I realized why I was the empathetic person I had always been. It was because of her. She was the strongest person I knew. Even though she was sick and weak, she was kind and helpful. At that moment, I embraced who I was and who I knew that I wanted to be.

If my mother would have only seen the problem, she would have missed the opportunity. In this negative, critical moment of sickness, the cloud of darkness that was holding me hostage lifted. I knew that I needed God to help me through. In the moment of sickness and treatments, my mother and I found the strength in enjoying the moments we had together. Without her cancer battle, we would have missed hours of time spent together.

You cannot pray in love but live in darkness. God wants you to be happy. God is big enough to comfort you and will calm you in your darkest hour. But you have to invite Him in. Remember, He is a gentleman and it is okay to ask God, "Where are you?" But do not rest in the idea of what you think is supposed to be, but rest in the process of knowing that God is in control.

I often found myself going to water when I needed a break from the darkness. I would visit the river when I needed to hear God speak clarity over my life. Mom was resting and I was struggling. So I went to the river and sat down on my normal rock, but it didn't feel right. The water wasn't moving that day. The water was still and dark in color and stinky in smell. I sat there feeling even more discouraged and confused. So I got up and moved down the river where I heard loud roaring water, traveling down a stream of twists and rocks. It was steadily moving; I felt the rapid movement that seemed to be led with anger and confusion. But I knew that is not what I had come for, so I kept moving. Finally, I heard the tranquility of the water. It was calm and peaceful, smooth yet steady. I stopped and sat down, knowing this is where I belonged on this day.

I felt as if God was showing me what I needed. If I would have stayed where I was comfortable and normal, I would have only experienced the negativity of still water that was dark and sad. If I wouldn't have kept moving until I found what I was needing and looking for, my experience would not have been the same. I would not have gotten out of the moment what I desperately needed. Do you ever feel like this in your life? You stay because it is where you usually go and where you feel most comfortable. Do you feel as if you can't keep moving because it is different from what you are used to?

This is where we grow skeptical of God's promises. If you don't keep moving and looking for what you need, you will stop growing in spirit and faith. Trust God will move you so that you can grow in Him. The river that day made me think of my life. The first body of water represented death. If my mother chose to not fight and to just stay there, that is what would have become. But because she spoke life into her situation, she kept moving and she accelerated. The water became to move a little more quickly, and like that, we pressed on. She did not press in to the season of disappointment, yet she pressed on to the season of hope and fight and she beat it!

The power of words is so inspirational. Do not use words of doubt and fear, but speak in faith and life. Your tongue is a good indicator of your spirit. If you speak life into your situation, then life will come out of it. During this season, I was beginning to learn this. Emotional scars take longer to heal and it takes great work, but I knew I was ready to overcome anything that came my way. My tongue is a condition of my heart and I was ready to move on following the word and love of Jesus.

Ask God to use you today. Repeat this prayer after me, "God, what do you need from me? I come to you in good favor and ask you to guide me in my life. Show me the goodness in people and the positive way in this journey. For you I live, and for you I will prevail. Use my tongue to encourage others and share your name. In Jesus's name, Amen."

I remember the day I whispered to God, "I found you, when I went looking for me..."

How big is your problem on a scale from 1 to God?

The problem	The truth	The lie you are believing	What does God say?

"Bear one another's burdens, and so fulfill
the law of Christ."

—Galatians 6:2

Soak in His Word and Share Your Thoughts!

CHAPTER 4

THE SEASON OF BROKENNESS

"He heals the brokenhearted and binds up
their wounds"
—Psalm 147:3

After hours of chemotherapy, countless trips to the doctor and
hospital, and five hours of surgery, my mother was in the season of healing. She had returned to her home and was even back to
work. We spoke multiple times a day, but she was doing well, and I
was so grateful. But now, I was faced with starting my life again. I was
still separated from my husband, twelve months had passed, and we
were both left with unanswered questions. So as I sat there my mind
wondered to *Now what, God?*

Have you ever felt that way? Overwhelmed with life, and you
look up and say, "Okay, I have done everything right and everything
I was supposed to...now what?" I was so thankful to God for healing
my mother, thankful for my husband to allow me the time to help
her, but now so much time had passed, what should I do? Do I forgive and forget or do I remain strong and move on with the divorce?
This question hung over me for weeks.

I remember waking up one morning, and I was unable to hide
my feelings. My emotional pain was pouring out, and physically, I
was wearing it. I had lost thirty pounds, and I was broken and felt
that I could get no relief. I continued to pray for complete healing
of my mother's body because I knew I needed her. I had allowed my
problems and my circumstances to weaken my confidence and self-

doubt was front and center in my thoughts. I was confident that after the divorce, we could start over. We had experienced so much hurt together that we needed a fresh start. I knew I needed to get in a state of spiritual and physical healing. But I had allowed others to destroy my confidence and was beginning to blame my life experiences for taking away my feeling of self-doubt and unworthiness.

Have you ever felt that way? One minute you feel on top of the world because you feel like you have everything in order. I like to compare it to a roller coaster of faith. One moment you are on top of the roller coaster. You are free and reaching out to God, smiling and strong. But in a split moment, life takes you down quickly. When you stop you are upside down, hanging on and praying for God to save you. You are scared and in need of Him again. You are so afraid you will fall. During these moments, we cling on to the word of God and His promises to protect us and His desire to love us.

Do you believe that in your most scared moment? Do you pray and praise Him the same that you do during your happy and good times? I didn't. I felt like I was using God and only talking to Him when I needed Him. What would happen if we did that to our friends? If you only spoke to them when you needed them or needed something. How would that make them feel? Or maybe you are thinking of a person like that right now. It is painful and it hurts. That is where I was in my marriage. I had made my husband stop his life and wait for me to decide what was going to happen to us. I had never been in control, and finally I was. But the longer I waited, I knew it was unfair, so I proceeded with the divorce.

The pain was pain, hurt, sadness, and fear. Have you ever experienced a pain or hurt that you cannot explain or even describe because you feel as if no one could possibly understand? God understands and He cares! He wants to be there for you! Each time I would pray during these dark days, I would hear the word *patience*. Okay, Lord, patience. But what do you do while you are waiting? I know that it is the hardest thing for me to do is to wait. What do you do in the waiting moment?

I continued to wait. I begged to hear from God, but I kept hearing patience. So that is what I would do until one night, I had found myself financially strapped and spiritually broken. It was a cold winter night, and I was physically cold. The windows had cracks in them, and I could see snowflakes flying in. I was lonely, scared, and hungry. I was lying on the dirty couch that was given to me in the mist of the nightmare. I was angry that I had left a warm, nice, and comfortable home, for this. I felt selfish that I was yet again, mad and confused with God. How could He want me to live like this? Why can't I just go home God? This is the moment I sat up, I threw my arms in the air, and as loud as I could, I screamed, "Lord, take this burden from me! Help me to see what you want me to do! I cannot make it on my own anymore. I am hungry, I can't pay rent, and my children need warm clothes." I heard nothing.

I closed my eyes, tears streaming down my face. I drifted off to sleep quickly. I saw my hands. They were the only things I could see against a black sky. I heard a voice say, "I gave these to you. Use them!" I woke up suddenly. I sat up and opened my eyes, but each time I closed them, I could see my hands. I closed my eyes, bowed my head, and said, "OK, God, I will use my hands, but guide me, Lord."

I got up and saw I had a message on my phone. It was from a lady that I had made hair bows for in the past. She was requesting I make hair bows for the local high school cheer squad and asked if I would be interested in making extra to sell at the cheer clinic being held later that week. I knew that I didn't have a lot of money to waste, but I went to the store and got the material I needed. With that order of hair bows, I had enough money to pay a bill and catch up.

I slowly began to post pictures of the items I was creating and making a few dollars here and there. I knew that rent was coming up and I still needed to buy groceries at the end of the week. But a lady from my church had asked me to make her a necklace. I didn't have the money, but I counted change to buy the needed material. I tucked the necklace in my purse and went to church the following Sunday morning. I found her before the service began and was saddened when she told me she didn't bring any money but would get it to me next week. I went ahead and gave her the necklace but was sickened with fear of what I was going to do.

The church service began, and I kept receiving a strong feeling to give. But I knew I didn't have it to give. When the offering bucket passed, I heard the words, "Give $5." I kept fighting off the words by thinking, *No! I only have $5, and that is going to get my children lunch.* But when it was time for the offering bucket to go back across my lap, I couldn't fight the urge and I placed my last $5 inside. I watched it get away from me and mixed in with other bills, some much larger than mine. I was scared and mad at myself for doing what I thought was a careless act.

After church, I smiled at others when I exited to my car and drove to pick up my children from their dad. We drove by McDonalds and they begged for a Happy Meal. I told them to please be patient and we would get it later in the week, but couldn't right now. But what they didn't know was that I didn't have enough money to buy them lunch. At that moment, my phone rang, and it was the lady from church. She asked if I could come to her house and pick up the money she owed me. I was filled with joy and proceeded to her home.

As I pulled into the lady's house I was so excited to get the $15 she owed me. She met me at her door, and she had an envelope waiting with my name on it. I thanked her and left. Once I got to the car, I opened the envelope, but much to my surprise, there was a crisp $100 bill inside. I immediately put the car back in park and went back to her door. She opened it with a smile and said that she had been given that money earlier in the month, but she felt like it didn't belong to her. She said she prayed over it, and it had sat there all month. On her way home from church that morning, she remembered the money and felt as if it belonged to me.

If I had not been obedient to God and His desire for me to sacrifice my last $5 for Him, I don't think He would have rewarded me with that money on that day! I had a need and He saw my need. He blessed me in such a way it changed everything that day. I was able to go to the grocery store and buy a weeks' worth of groceries, along with two Happy Meals, and still had some left over.

At that moment, I realized that my whole life I had been living it alone. Not physically alone, but spiritually alone. I didn't fully trust

Him until that moment. I finally gave Him something to work with. He has always been there, but I didn't allow Him to work in my life. I wasn't believing in His peace and His grace that only He can offer and bless. I was broken. I was tired and I needed Him, and He knew I was finally ready to see His love and commitment.

We can have peace in each season, even the broken season. But you must trust in Him. If you truly connect with God, you will be filled with peace. You can cultivate an intimacy with God, and once you feel that unforgiving peace, you will want to make it a lifestyle. This is where prayer comes in. Praying can be intimidating. I was afraid to do it wrong. I felt as if I was being punished for not being able to pray or translate to Him through prayer. I was lacking confidence that only I can find.

Do you know that God knows everything about you? He hears the words spoken in your head and the grunts in your sleep. He loves you. He is there for you. He does not leave you, and He does not forsake you.

I want you to stop right now and say this prayer, "Lord God, I want to reflect your goodness, Father. I want to act like you. I want to mock your goodness and ask that you give me visions so that I can model how to be more like you. Amen."

Moments with God has taught me to be content. Look unto Him when you are weak. When you surrender it all, you will gain His everything. He can and will bring wholeness to a broken heart. I wanted to feel complete within myself again. I could not do it without remaining faithful in my journey with God. Do not look back, move forward, and you will see what He holds for you.

It is important to express the raw truth of your situation to the one that holds it all. With Him, you should feel no shame. There is no shame in being tired. We are all tired and we all come to a time in our lives when we are broken beyond earthly repair. That is when you know that you are spiritually tired and you need the grace of God that only He can mend. He will reach out His hand of mercy that is needed to heal your soul. When you are in this state of emotional despair, you need to listen to your soul. Every decision that is led by stress can be a struggle, and each conversation feels as if it is a crumbling wall. You need to take time of deep rest. You are more than the darkness that you face.

During this season, shame kept cresting. Shame for being angry at God for allowing this dreadful disease to grow inside of my mother and for the devil to clasp on to my marriage. When you feel shame, it makes you feel helpless. I felt shame for being upset with my mom that I had devoted my last year to make sure she was healthy and now my failing marriage is still a mess and even closer to divorce than ever before. But I also felt shame that I would even think that I had any other option. I would have been there for my mom no matter the circumstance.

This is when I decided to put on my armor. If I have on my God armor, no one person, not my thoughts or my fears can stop me. I am His and He is mine. If you don't expect disappointment, you will be shook. I continued to ask for peace and His guidance. I did not lean on my own understanding of why my mother had cancer or why she had it during my most difficult season of life. But instead, I began to celebrate our time we had together.

I watched a woman whom I always considered to be weak, to rise against the darkest storm and she looked the devil in the eye, and she won. She was fierce and she was strong. She showed me that if you have the desire to fight with God in your corner, nothing could stop you. We shared more meals together in that year that we had in the past ten years. We held hands and shared more hugs that I had ever remembered sharing. My mother shared stories from her past that I never knew she had even experienced.

Once I decided to not let anger speak to me, but instead, I allowed life to shine through. I then spoke with confidence instead of doubt. I was no longer disappointed by the world, but I was able to show the world how I handled it with grace and God. I was able to be still and listen, and I knew my chapter was not over and neither was my mother's. She had a result in her mind, and she spoke to that. She created the end goal to be to meet her grandson and to spend the summer at the beach and Disney with her grandbabies and her daughters. She expected it and she received the blessing.

During this season, I was taught that even if the storm is raging, you can still celebrate in the storm and you can dance in the rain. When you are afraid of getting wet, instead of embracing the cool and refreshing experience, you will miss so much. I challenge you during this time of soaking in the Lord's work, that you embrace the "not so perfect days" and think of the goodness of the moment or day. I always would tell my mom, "Yes, it is difficult, but it could be so much worse!"

Remember, God is writing our story. He is there to help guide us through the storm. He cries with us, and He knows that it is not easy. But with his forgiving grace, we make it through, and with much surprise, we come out stronger, happier, and appreciative. This is when perspective comes into play. Life is how we look at it. It is our choice to sit and sulk or to stand up and praise. Do you want to allow the devil to control your decision, or do you want to confess to be cleansed? This will allow you to be set free and break from the bondage of the ugly, broken, and sinful parts of your situation and self.

> "As for God, His way is perfect: The Lords word is flawless; He shields all who take refuge in Him."
>
> —Psalm 18:30

What situation happened to you that broke you?

_____

_____

_____

_____

Ask God, "Where were you?"

_____

_____

_____

_____

Or "Where are you?
How will I make it across this?"

_____

_____

_____

_____

Soak in His Word and Share Your Thoughts!

CHAPTER 5

THE SEASON OF UNCERTAINTY

"Love the Lord your God with all your heart
and with all your soul and with all your mind."
—Matthew 22:37

Divorce. I cannot even begin to give my definition of the word. Some nights I would ask myself, is there a different between death and divorce? Is the pain, loneliness, and sadness any different? I would begin to question every decision I had ever made up to this point. I was so curious about my purpose, my plan, and my path after divorce. Have you ever felt curious about your decisions? Curious about a life event that is happening to you and no one else? Curious about life in general.

What is my purpose? Where are you, God? Just like children, we adults feel curiosity. We too must nurture that feeling, and when you do, you will feel satisfaction and more complete in your journey. Life can make us very curious, and in order to grow, you must nurture these thoughts.

During my journey, I had touched on a variety of emotions. The one that stayed with me most of the way was uncertainty. Even with the help of the Lord, I was confused, angry, and hungry for more understanding. I could not understand how my journey of lies, deception, cancer, and divorce were given to me. But at this point of my spiritual journey, I didn't feel alone. I felt His presence and I pressed in to Him with each step I took. I knew He was in control and He would show His presence when I needed it.

There have been moments when I felt life was throwing stones at me. No matter how hard I try, it hurts. You protect yourself with the armor of God. Get up and rise above the conflict you are facing. You must collect the rocks (conflicts) with confidence and begin to build a wall with everything you have collected and been through. Sometimes the harsh truths cannot be hidden. But you can stand up and show others that strength, independence, and growth can be created out of the damages we once experienced.

Goodness still exists and you must take the courage to break the negative patterns using God. If the path that you are on does not serve you in goodness and positivity, they do not belong to you. Break free. Give yourself the permission you need to stop and reflect. Take care of yourself. It is okay! You are not selfish; you are so loved that you need to be okay in order to help others. Life does not need to be any more complicated than it already can be. I speak life into my situations and simplicity. With speaking the positive words into my life and situation, I am reminding myself of such things. Abraham Lincoln said it best, "We can complain because rose bushes have thorns or rejoice because thorn bushes have roses." The choice is yours.

I was once told, "Turn your pain, into a purpose." More often times than not, a person does not have the energy or desire to do that. At this point, I had been given so much I felt as if there was no other way than to keep moving forward, and by doing so, I would be able to find my purpose. I started this process by trying to reexamine the word *love*. Before divorce, I could quickly define *love* by smiling and saying it is a feeling of happiness. At this moment, *love* was really hard to define. My perception of love and the reality of love is not the same as it was before.

I would look for the problem within me, I tried to change, but when I did, I still couldn't make the situation better. That is not love. Love is patient, and love is truly kind. Love is not something that we need to search for or beg to receive that feeling from another human being. I have realized that love comes from above and then shines from within. This is where the Bible says, "Come and have abundant life." Do you have abundance in your life? Promise to not ever lose yourself again but only learn more and more ways to love God, your-self, and others.

It can take a while to get to this point of confidence. But I have learned that when you are worried about someone not liking you, remember, it is none of your business or concern if that person likes you or not. It is only your business or concern if you allow it to impact you in a negative way. Words are powerful, but they only hold the amount of power that we allow. If you continue your journey and allow the past to continue to hurt you and have a negative impact on your life, day, or season. You are still choosing to allow that person to hurt you. You will be making a choice to be stuck in suffering and not rejoicing like God desires and encourages us to do.

All we have is this very moment, please don't waste it. Stop what you are doing, and I am going to give you a challenge. Think about a person that you want to make a positive impact in their life. This could be someone that you know or a complete stranger. I challenge you to call them, leave them a note, text them, or smile at them. Do this for thirty days. Once you do this for thirty days, it will become a habit. Be kind, feel kind, and show kindness.

Allow God to release you. Forgive the past and trust the future. If you have to do this daily, say it daily. "Lord, I forgive the past, and I trust in the future." Surrender the negative thoughts and feelings you once had against another, or a situation and be obedient. It is a choice, not a feeling. I did not enjoy the season of uncertainty, and I knew that I could declare the change. Remember all works together for Good. It states that in the Bible, women want to be loved and men want to be respected. Be the seed planter in your relationship or situation. Be respectful and love will be in return. When I say that, I mean God. Show God the respect and He will show you His love, grace, and mercy like no one else has shown you. As the season of uncertainty was coming to a close, without my knowledge of course. I was told by my preacher that I must trust in the Lord and allow Him to be my husband. At this moment, I needed reassurance that this could be possible. I began pray and believe that He would provide for my children and I, love me like a husband would, and respect me when I needed space. I truly did not understand how this could possibly be, but I didn't question, I didn't resist, I opened my heart and my mind to this possibility.

I knew there would be moments when I would question: Will I ever be happy again? Will I get back to normal? Will I ever be who I was before divorce? Before I allowed God to step in my life and be my husband, all of those answers were so far out of reach and dark. Not until I realized that only if you have happiness will it add happiness into your life. Moments add value to your life and make you a happier, better, and healthier person. But you don't need another person to help you understand this. You don't need another person to tell you how great you are. You need to allow God to be that person. Allow Him to fill that goodness inside of your heart so that you will never forget how it truly feels to be loved.

I realized that the moments that I felt weak, ashamed, and unworthy was because I wasn't strong enough to save myself from the shame and doubt. I was weak and unable to fight the inner battles without God. The constant feeling of empathy and living my life to please others had taken everything that I had. The moment you let go of the fear of bothering everyone you come into contact with, and the moment that you stop avoiding conversations, you are set free from the strongholds of the devil.

Do not struggle with these burdens alone anymore. Speak against the feelings and words others are telling you or what you are thinking about yourself. I want you to fill this out right now.

I speak against the feeling of_____

_____.

You will not control me anymore!

I speak against the feeling of_____

_____.

You will not control me anymore!

Do this as many times as you need to, until you believe it. Stop believing the lies and stand up for the truth in which God gave you. You are not broken, you are *beautiful*; you are not a mess, you are a *masterpiece*; you are not weak, you are *strong*; you are not poor, you are *rich* in His kingdom! If you speak truth and life over your situation, your situation and your life *will* change. I challenge you to do this for the next thirty days! You must command: I am a blessed. I am blessed to be a blessing to others. Remember He saved you from something for something. Now, you must seek to get better and know you are a light in this dark place! Go shine!

God has saved me from _____

_____

_____

_____

God has saved me from _____

_____

_____

_____

Do this as many times as you need. Write it, read it, repeat it.

"He heals the wounds of every shattered heart"

—Psalm 147:3

Soaking in the Word

Date:

Verse:

Thoughts:

Prayers:

Praises:

Soak in His Word and Share Your Thoughts!

CHAPTER 6

THE SEASON OF OBEDIENCE

> "But blessed is the one who trusts in the
> Lord, whose confidence is in Him."
> —Jeremiah 17:7

Doubt. When you are in doubt, you worry, and it is a starting point. Worry is simply a lack of trust in God. Think about worrying as a metaphor, your grandma sitting in her rocking chair. She is moving back and forth, back and forth without stopping, but she never goes anywhere. The rocking chair remains in the same place, and it doesn't let her move forward. If you are insecure about your situation, take your eyes off the problem, and place your eyes on God and His promise. Having insecurities is an act of selfishness. Speak out to the worry or the insecurity. Speak yes and Amen. Speak peace in the situation.

At this point in my life, I was full of doubt and worry. Doubting my decision-making process, my emotions, and my purpose. I knew that everything that had happened to me, up to this point in my life, was my race. I knew that Jesus was there, but when you allow doubt in, you will begin to waiver and question the word. Doubt allows us to question the goodness of God's glory and grace. When you allow doubt in, you have allowed the devil to take away your faith. We have each been given an amount of faith. It is up to us to take that faith and expand it. Faith grows and expands. I wasn't doing that. I was allowing self-pity and pain to control my days. When I allowed doubt to enter my thoughts, I was speaking doubt, and my faith disappeared.

Have you ever asked yourself, what is your perception of Jesus? Our faith is limited on our reality. If your need is not met in prayer, was it a true need in God's eyes? You must believe He desires to answer your prayers. If you question His position in your problem, you will have no stability in that problem or situation. Do not dismiss Him. Do not question Him. It is in His perfect timing. Perception isn't reality. Perception is the ability to become aware of something through our senses. Reality is the world or the state of things as they actually exist. Whatever the Lord asked you to do, He will also make you available and able to accomplish is.

Do you believe in truth and faith or do have unbelief? Do you ever get misleading information? Once you receive this misleading information, you can start believing it, and it can become your reality. Do you ever make a decision, only on misleading information that was given to you, and ask why was I so blind after you look back at the event? Why was my heart so hard? So unwilling to change in that moment? My question to you is, did you pray about it, or did you go with the information that was given? Honor Him and He will honor you. If you feel like you can't do it, you are not running your race. Give it to Him and wait. Stay in your lane, and your daily battles will get lighter.

Do you ever feel like Job? I feel like Job all the time. I have been told many, many times that I have patience like Job. I do have the patience like he, but I also feel like I can relate to him in a much deeper level. I have experienced the feeling of loss. Job knows how it feels to have a precious gift taken away in one moment. Life is frail, free of uncertainties, full of frustration. But, you must understand, how short and uncertain life truly is? We do not want to live in fear of death, but this is where we want abundant life.

I must ask, have you ever experienced grief? Grief can be the death of a relative, friend, or pet. It is the act of losing someone. If the answer is yes, know that your grieving and your pain is recorded. God has watched and collected your pain and your tears. Have you ever had to ask Him, "Where were you, God?" If so, know that you need to invite Him in. Remember he has recorded my story, He knows my sorrow and my weakness. But this is where you must trust Him, depend on Him.

When I soak on the word of God, I find myself going to my mom's first cancer battle. I often find myself going to the verse in Romans 8:28, "God promises to make something good out of the storms that bring devastation to your life." It makes me think, maybe my mom was assigned this mountain to show me it could be moved. She spoke life, and she fought. She was strong, but she got tired. She had fallen, but she had not failed. She was broken, but with God, she rose up again. She was healed and she did overcome.

This is when you must ask yourself, are you being useful or useless in your journey? Do you blend in or do you want to stand up and stand out to show others God's glory? Are you adding positivity and joy to other's lives? I want people to see me and think that I am different, and because of that, they see the reflection of Jesus within me. Sharing goodness and kindness to others. A simple act could be to open the door for another, offer a hand at the grocery store, or take a couple of seconds out of your busy, rushed day and allow the car you have seen been passed by ten cars pull out in front of you.

Okay, I am going to be real for a moment. Have you ever done that, and you felt so good about yourself for letting them out in front of you and then they don't wave or honk or even nod their head at you! Oh my word! I used to get so mad, mumble under my breath, and then take it out on the next person I see trying to pull out. But now, I will simply say a prayer for the person who did not show a symbol of appreciation. You must remember maybe that small amount of curtesy or respect is all they have had or all they have seen in a long time, if ever. Maybe by doing this small act, you are showing the reflection of God. Do not stay in the season of doubt. Let go of the burdens you are holding on to. One way of letting go of the burdens is to pray and trust in God.

Do you realize that prayer is the most important conversation of the day? Take it to God before you take it to anyone else. This is a very important and hard lesson for many of us to learn, but especially it was for me. Privacy is powerful and should be valued. What people do not know about you, they cannot take away from you. This is important to remember when you feel as if you need to talk about what you are dealing with or going through. You must ask yourself, have you prayed about it as much as you have talked about it? If God has opened doors to put down a problem, person, or situation, do not pick it back up, if God told you to put it down. You can still be kind and patient and still be allowed to say no. Think back to where you started and see where you are now. You can be in an entirely different place emotionally, physically, financially, and mentally. But you cannot give up on your situation or yourself. Keep working, keep moving, and keep believing in you. You are changed because you are loved by God. You are strong and unstoppable because you are loved by God.

At this point, you must show God that you are learning your self-worth. It is okay to tell people no. When you give yourself to everyone else, what is left for you? Do not overcommit and allow God to work in you. Delight in Him and get your needs from Him. Be excited about life each and every day. "You have not, because you ask not." Choose love, choose God; and with Him, you are choosing inner health. Do not allow the fear of failing control again.

"Mold me, shape me, until I think like you Lord."

—Romans 12:2

What is your need right now?

↓

[ ]

What tools do you need to be obedient to God?

[ ]

↙   ↓   ↘

| Step 1 | Step 2 | Step 3 |

_____   _____   _____

_____ → _____ → _____

_____   _____   _____

Soak in His Word and Share Your Thoughts!

_____

_____

_____

_____

_____

_____

_____

_____

_____

_____

_____

_____

_____

_____

_____

_____

_____

_____

_____

_____

_____

_____

_____

_____

_____

_____

_____

_____

_____

CHAPTER 7

THE SEASON OF PRAISE

"Pray and never give up."

—Luke 18:1

Like always, life kept moving. It was a normal Friday and my children and I had a movie date. We had been very excited for this movie, we had discussed what candy we were going to purchase and what soda we would be drinking. We showed up to the theater eager and ready to enjoy. Much to my surprise, the movie that was supposed to last two hours was stopped short about an hour in. I had my phone on silent, and I kept seeing a strange number calling. I ignored it once, then twice, but after the third time, I knew I needed to step out.

Have you ever heard someone say, "That phone call that changed my life?" Yeah, that was what happened to me. When I answered the phone, that very moment, life stopped. I could hear my mother on the other end, sobbing. I couldn't understand her, I kept asking her to calm down, take a breath. "Are you OK?" I kept asking. Suddenly a strange voice came on the phone. The voice was soft and calm, and all I remember hearing was, "Cancer is back...tumors... your mom needs you."

I couldn't breathe. I couldn't think. I dropped the phone, only to pick it up quickly to find out where she was and how long it would take me to get to her. It was a long, lonely, and confusing drive to the hospital that was over an hour away. I kept replaying the words, and I was sure they were confused. How could an ER doctor tell my healthy mom that she has cancer again? I remember walking through the unfamiliar doors of the hospital. I walked up and told the receptionist who I was and who I needed to see. I was quickly greeted by the doctor. Again I found myself in a long, white, and cold hallway. Alone with the doctor who said your mother came in with back pain, and they had performed an MRI. She said, "We found two tumors on her spine and a mass in her lung...I am so sorry." Sorry? I didn't want to hear sorry, I wanted to hear a plan. A path of wellness.

Walking into that room was a moment I wish I wouldn't have to have in my memory. Seeing her sitting there, scared and alone. We met eyes, and tears streamed down both of our cheeks. This moment was different from the first time. She wasn't speaking life over her situation; she looked at me, and she was tired. She said, "Morgan, I can't go through this again." I of course, said, "Yes, you will, and yes, you can!" She closed her eyes and she began to pray. The doctor came in to a quiet room to find us asking the simple question, "What do we do next?" She gave me a couple of phone numbers and sent us out the door. Yet again, I packed Mom in my car, made arrangements to have her car picked up, and we went to my house. I quickly began making phone calls, scheduling appointments, and getting time off work.

The day came for more tests, followed by more and more. Each day, she grew weaker, paler, and ate less. I just couldn't figure out why God was allowing this to happen. I received a phone call a few days after the tests and was asked if I could bring my mom in to her oncologist the following day. I knew this was not a positive sign since she had just had her brain scan the day prior. I tried to stay optimistic, and we talked, she slept, and we joked on our drive. Only to find out my mother had not only tumors on her spine and a mass in her lung, but she had it throughout her body and it had made it to her brain.

Again, I needed a plan. What was the next step, where do I take her, who is going to help my mom? The only answer was for her to be admitted in the hospital to get her pain under control. Again, I loaded her in the car and drove her to my local hospital upon her request. That is where my mom stayed for one week, until she was released to a hospice center. She was in the hospice center for two days before she went home to be with my dad, her mom, dad, and brother. But something I think about often is the last week I had with my mom.

The stories and the what if's. In the moment of pain, hurt, and sorrow. I was blessed with conversations that not many people can share with their loved ones before they perish. We spoke about Jesus and who would be there to greet her upon arrival to heaven. "Do you think your dad will be happy to see me?" she asked one night. I giggled, and said, "Without a doubt, he will be pushing everyone out of the way to kiss his sweetheart!" We held hands a lot. I gave my mother baths up to the day it was too painful. I was scared. Scared of so many things, but the one thing that was most frightful was not having her. What would I do? Who would I call? And all the memories she would miss of her grandbabies, which she loved so much.

But with all these negative thoughts, I felt peace. I felt His presence, His love, and His desire to make my mom healthy in heaven. I gave my questions and my fears to the one who had not left me, who had not forsaken me during this difficult time. He gave me the strength to climb in bed with my mom and hold her after she had went home. The tears streaming down my face were not only tears of hurt and sadness but of praise and love. She was not in pain. She was not gasping for her next breath. She was released from this terrible disease which took my mom from my sister and me in three short weeks. I was blessed by a loving mother and father. That is something not everyone can say, and I know I was blessed.

In moments of sadness, do you feel like you have just experienced a storm? Ask yourself, why did I survive? How did I survive? In this moment, I knew God had positioned me for this moment. He had prepared me for my mother's death. He could have taken her the first time, but he knew I needed her. When God is in your everyday life, you are more aware of Him and the moments where He is. I am thankful for my connection with God and my trust I have in Him.

Death. What a hard season it becomes when death enters. You must be courageous. Courageous of what is expected of you and what you will have to face. In the moment, you will not know what is next, but with His love and grace, He will guide you. Without Him, I was hostage in my own life, but I am not broken anymore. I believe in myself and in my God.

God so desperately needs and craves your attention. When God kept speaking patience over my life, in the moment I was confused and frustrated. But now when I think of the word *patience*, I think of power. What a strong and powerful word it is to me. When I pray about my home, my finances, and allowing others in my life, I continue to hear patience. This is when I trust in Him. I trust in His words and His plans He has for me. Everything will come to me when He is ready to bless me. Everything He is preparing me for is good. The next chapter is here. Embrace your season, and write your story. My challenge for you is to choose a person and pray for them, without letting them know. Just sit and wait. Wait to see the positive change in that person's life and blessings they will receive without even knowing that you are praying for them.

Praise God in advance even on your dark day or dark moment. Praise will take possession of my problem or moment. Trust God even when the answer is wait. You are not unwanted; you are chosen. You are not unloved; He died for *you*! You are never alone; you are His!

> "God promises to make something good out of the storms that bring devastation to your life."
>
> —Romans 8:28

Soak in His Word and Share Your Thoughts!

CHAPTER 8

THE SEASON OF TRUST

"For I know the plans I have for you," declares the LORD, "plans to prosper you and not to harm you, plans to five you hope and a future."

—Jeremiah 29:11

Are you full of happiness, peace, and joy? Do you feel contentment in your life? Did you know contentment is a choice? Thankfulness leads to contentment. Put God first and the peace will then flow into your life. Do you count your blessings or the blessings of others? This is when you must trust God. Trust Him that He knows where you belong in your journey. We need His presence, not His presents. Do you ever ask Jesus what you need? Thank Him for what you do have? Or are only complaining about what you don't have?

You must not be afraid while you are in your season of trust. "Everyone is created for a purpose beautifully." But what happens when you feel like you have been given the wrong answer to a question? Is the answer you received wrong or just not what you wanted to hear? This is when you must put trust in your life, your decisions, and your God. If you are allowing others to influence you, then you are not living for God. Pray, ask God, and wait for His answer. He will not give you bad answers, He will be innocent and intentional. If you have allowed others to give you answers, and now you are working on that bad answer, you ask, "Where do I go from here?"

You must have an open heart to have an open mind. When you give God your experiences and your situation, do you refuse Him? Do you hear Him? Allow your time to be intimate, loving, and quiet. I sometimes think back and realize I was living in a constant state of chaos. I was confused, empty, and scared. You must remember you don't owe God anything. You can ask for everything, but you don't need to give Him anything except your obeisance. He desires you.

Do you ever love someone or something so much you question, can I love too much? Do you expect something from someone that is too much for them? When you don't know the other person's expectations, you can't or won't make sense or understand their disappointment. My faith gives me the expectations I need, and I want to make that contagious to everyone I meet. I feel like as a Christian; we can be given a lot of pressure. Pressure from the outside world and within. I know as I was going through my divorce, I felt so much pressure. Pressure to make the right decision for my family as a whole, myself, my children, and my husband. If I was given the same decision and same pressure today that I felt those years ago, I am confident that I would make a different decision. I made decisions on worldly comments, instead of inviting God into the conversation. My expectations of my husband were not realistic and I allowed my own disappointments to control my emotions. We do not want to allow ourselves to get to this point.

We must trust in Him, even in the no. When God is working, it is worth the wait. During this time, God will allow you to recognize things you may have been too busy to see before. If God removes someone from your life and their absence brings you peace, this is when you realized you needed to release them. Being imperfect is OK. We are told to act and look a certain way by society, but in God's eyes, we are strong. We do not have to be perfect to be saved by His perfect Grace. The day I realized that I could turn my worry and fear into worship and praise is the very day my battles became blessings. This is not your whole book; it is only a sentence. Keep moving, and He will keep providing.

God has put a promise in you. Together God wants to help you work on this promise. Do not get discouraged if life is not happening on your timeline. Keep praying and keep believing. He has not forgotten that promise. Shake free from your shames, no matter how dark and live in the desire He shares with you. "For I know the plans I have for you declares the Lord. Plans to prosper and not to harm you, plans to give you hope and a future" (Jeremiah 29:11). Your strength is your own belief. Sometimes, God will bypass what you prayed for to give you what you really need in that moment.

When you make the decision to live in faith instead of fear, your self-awareness recognizes the lies that you have become to believe about yourself. You no longer look at what others think of you, but you only focus on how God sees you. Call each fear and lie by name. Even if the lies feel real and the fear is realistic, speak to it.

What is a lie you believe about yourself? Take time to think about it.

The Lie	The Truth	Supporting Bible Verse

If you know Jesus, your lie or fear is not permanent. Have faith. Have you ever felt unclean because of a decision you have made? Because of actions, thoughts, or words from another. Our Jesus does not judge. We are all clean in His eyes if we reach for Him and ask for forgiveness of our sins. When He died for you on the cross, He took payment for all the sins we have committed, thought about, or will commit. He is a forgiving Father. And when you are touched by His goodness, everything will be wiped away. You will be made to feel free and clean. Make the decision right now to be healed from the lies of the enemy and be set free of your sin.

I think back to the moment when my mother knew she wasn't going to be healed physically, she smiled and knew with confidence she was being healed spiritually. She rededicated her life to her Lord and savior. She was at peace and was beautiful. Days before her death, she had shared with me a vision she had had of Jesus in her hospital room. She described Him in a white robe with His arms reached out. She said, "Morgan, He wanted me to come with Him then, but I wasn't ready." Those conversations are something that no one can take from me and something that will never be replaced.

When she passed away, she was looking up toward her father in heaven, and it was beautiful. She left me with faith and peace, teaching me a lesson: if you trust and love God, He will not leave you or forsake you. Days are still hard and moments are still emotional, but in those moments, I pray and ask for God's grace and blessings. I receive them, willingly and openly. Grace is a free gift He offers, and we must not take advantage nor forget. Reach out, grab it, and don't let go.

There was a moment that I once would have been angry at God, for taking away my only living parent. I would have been angry for the way she struggled the last week of her life. But this time was different. As I lay there in the bed, holding the woman who had once held me, I felt peace and love. I felt a calming sense of life and energy. I was thankful that God was there with me at that moment, and that I had not walked away from Him like I had in all the hard times in my past. He was there for me. I could feel Him. I spoke God's promise to my mountain, and it was moved. The hurt and torture the devil was putting on my mother was crushed by God. I had living faith that His faith would overcome the dead in my life, and He would show me the freedom of death instead of the hurt and fear.

Do you have a mountain that you want moved? No problem is too small compared to our Lord. If you have enough faith, the same amount as the mustard seed, you can move anything you need moved. Do not have unbelief in your life or situation, and do not give in to the faithless generation in which we are walking with. If you have unbelief in your heart, ask Him right now to help, Lord, in my unbelief, I overcome this fear and I believe. Command your mountain to move.

My mountain at this moment was the preparing of my mother's funeral service. With the help and guidance of my sister, aunt, and uncle, I was able to make the decisions that needed made. My mother was what some call claustrophobic. She did not like tight spaces and did not like to get too hot. She told me fifteen years ago when my father died that she would want to be cremated. It was an ongoing joke that I would not do that to her unless it was in writing. The week she was in the hospital, she wrote it down and underlined it a lot! So I did just that.

We had a visitation, which she did not want to have, but she didn't want me to spend the money on it. But she deserved it, and she had almost six hundred people in attendance in a three-hour span. She was so loved and respected. Her service was beautiful, and she would have been so proud of my sister and me. But because my sister lived so far away and my dad was gone, I had to start the process of cleaning out her home.

This is when I needed to have trust in my season and my journey. I wasn't going through my mom's items, but I was going through my parent's items, at the young age of thirty-four. Days were long, and moments were sad. But I did it, and I know it was because I had Jesus. He didn't leave me and He didn't forsake me. The selling process was quick and painless. Life was finally getting back to my new normal.

"I will bless the Lord at all times, His praise
shall continually be in my mouth."
—Psalm 34:1

Soak in His Word and Share Your Thoughts!

CHAPTER 9

THE SEASON OF FAITH

"God is faithful, and He will not let you be
tested beyond your strength."
—1 Corinthians 10:13

During my journey, my faith has given me expectations.
Expectations of what I expect from myself and others. I started
my journey of breaking free in the season of empathy. Before I allowed
God to be present in my day, I felt unworthy. I felt unloved. But
now, I feel beautiful and strong and valued. I need you to remember,
"Once your self-esteem is distorted, you get defensive." I now wake
up with God on my mind. I spend time soaking in His word. I have
the confidence that if I walk into a dark season, I will light it up
because of Him. The sequence of my life might not make sense, but
because of His grace and mercy, I will be OK! I have potential and I
was created for a great purpose.

I thank God for all He has done for me, and I tell Him what I
need. Pray to God for peace. It is important to remember that not
all battles come to disrupt your life and not all come from the devil.
Some come by and with the grace of God. The decisions that we
make, whether right or wrong, can then be used by God to clear your
way and open your heart to something you are missing. Happy is the
person who learns to wait as you pray. Happy is the one who never
loses patience. We focus on our own feelings, and in these moments,
Jesus wants us to not pay mind to how we are feeling but to focus our
attention on His truth.

I would like to encourage you to always encourage others. Stay brave, humble, and support others. I believe that I was sent out into this world in hopes to serve others and open doors. When you feel that you are in the darkness, do not allow the dark, sad thoughts to sit and keep you in the dark. Do not be afraid to speak them out loud. Give God the power to hear your needs and release to Him. Stop allowing fear of getting it wrong to stop you from trying. If you never allow fear to leave your heart or situation, then how can it be eliminated? Words are powerful and God has given you an ability to speak power into your life with words. During experiences, have powerful insight and expectations for yourself. Do you expect power from yourself?

When God made me, He created uniqueness. Do not deny who you are, and who you are made to be. I refuse to let anyone decide who I am or who will control me. I have lived through some ugly stuff, and I do not want to ignore that. The ugly stuff has assisted in create who I am, and you cannot leave behind the past. Don't stop, just grow from it. When I think of my life, I think of surviving the losses, to be able to appreciate the thrives! If you can keep your head up, then the hardship and extreme trauma that you have conquered will not stare you in the face, but it will help steer you to where you want to be.

Please remember, your strength is your own belief. Speak to make yourself happy, do not speak to impress others. Do everything with a good, kind heart, and expect nothing in return and you will never be disappointed. Sometimes the smallest step in the right direction ends up being the biggest step of your life. And in the end, all I have learned was how to be strong, alone with God and in His hesitation. Within that hesitation, you will find your answer and your calling. Allow Him to transform your life.

Are you going to allow the next season to be a disappointment or a blessing? When you don't get something that you want or worked for, do you trust that it is a blessing or a disappointment? Guard and protect your position and He will protect you. Do you have a higher priority than the purpose you have created? God's promises are optional. Thinking about your current situation, what do you see?

Fill out the situation you are focusing on now. Circle the word that best describes the situation. Take time and pray about the word and write what comes to mind.

Bitterness	Deliverance
Sadness	Happiness
Joy	Hardship
Disappointment	Blessing
Forgiveness	Freedom
Faith	Fear
Blessing	Burden

Remember that the enemy does not steal your glory all at once. He will do it, little by little. Don't stop at the edge of the promise of God, keep going. Do not run from something that God has already defeated. Do not keep asking for something to be removed when God has left it. Whatever is left in your life, that you are blaming the devil, maybe God left it to help you in your situation. Never forget who got you from Point A to Point B.

Remember that no matter the reason or the season you are in, embrace the nos. The nos will give you a power you didn't know existed. He may not have given you relief in the situation, but He gave you grace. He leaves weaknesses in your life, only for those weakness to lead you to your strength. Praise Him for your problems because maybe those problems are there to protect you. He will be with you if you allow Him to be. Choose to follow God. Allow gradual change to occur so that you don't get too prideful, and remain faithful to Him. Put your problems beneath God and they can never hurt you. The favor of God opens doors. The enemy will come to distract you, but do not allow him to do so. Do not feel defeated because you are distracted. Allow God to be your audience and no one else. When you do not feel valued, appreciated, or abandoned, look to Him. Do not live for approval of others and know God loves you in every season. God bless you in your next race!

I need you to take a moment and ask yourself a few questions: Do you satisfy your desires with others, or do you allow God to satisfy you? This is the season I am walking in right. I have made it past self-hatred. I do not numb myself with empty pleasures. I do not get validation from others. I no longer feel trapped. I do not feel trapped by others, by lies, or by shame. The moment I gave my life to God, I was set free.

Now my life and my journey with God is up to me. That is why each and every day is important, and the investment I put into my relationship with God is number one. I speak truth in and over *my* life. *I* am choosing to walk in spiritual freedom. God will bless my free will. I will not allow my grief of my parents and the grief of my failed marriage to lead me in a sinful life or a life of lost desires. I have love for myself and a redemption in my heart for my Creator, and it feels good.

As this book comes to an end. I want to leave you with thoughts and challenges for yourself. I want you to ask yourself these questions: What level of character are you? What is your level of honesty?

You have a responsibility to God and yourself to be loyal and truthful. In the past I would lie to please others. I would lie to make them happy. If I would have told the truth about what I thought or what I wanted, my truth would have not brought them happiness. So instead, I lived in lies, and that made my life hell. I was pretending to be someone I was not...for what? For whom? Not God and not for me.

This is not okay to do. You have a voice. You have a choice. You are important! Do you feel free in your life? Or are you trapped? If you feel trapped, stop and break free from the bondage. If you allow God to show up and love you and provide for you, feel His love. You will feel hope, faith, and freedom.

Be intentional in your walk with God. Connect with Him, and after you do, each action will be full of godly intentions. Be disciplined. Do not wake up and grab your phone. Open your eyes and give God the glory to be alive one more day. Pray and spend time with Him. Be still and invite Him in your life, your day. Receive His love and love who He made you to be.

I want to leave you with some important moments and knowledge.

- You do not own your loved ones. Remember who gave them to you. Do not bring ownership in your home.
- The devil will always try to separate you from your solution.
- Every word you speak is either speaking life or death. Your words have meaning. What are you reflecting?
- One of the most powerful things you have been given is your story, your testimony.
- The power to do what we need to do only comes from Him.
- Learn from your past. Do not allow it to be where you remain.
- Very few things can be as liberating as forgiveness (1 Corinthians 15).
- Are you going to look at your situation or circumstance through the eyes of fear or faith?
- I choose faith and God's freedom.

"I have goodness and love in my heart."
—Psalm 23:6

Praise Report

What is going good right now?

_____
_____
_____
_____
_____
_____

Do you feel like you are growing closer to
God? Tell Him! Praise be to God.

_____
_____
_____
_____
_____

Soak in His Word and Share Your Thoughts!

About the Author

Morgan Nucilli is an author, energetic trainer, and child advocate. Morgan uses her energy to encourage adults and children to live their life to the fullest. She is motivational and inspirational. Morgan is authentic and reaches people with her down-to-earth personality and real-life experiences. Morgan believes everyone has a story and everyone deserves to be heard. Morgan resides in West Virginia with her two children.

CPSIA information can be obtained
at www.ICGtesting.com
Printed in the USA
BVHW030259151220
595774BV00013B/63